T0193218

Vietnam Did It

LARRY LONG

WESTBOW
PRESS®
A DIVISION OF THOMAS NELSON
& ZONDERVAN

WestBow Press books may be ordered through booksellers or by contacting:

WestBow Press
A Division of Thomas Nelson & Zondervan
1663 Liberty Drive
Bloomington, IN 47403
www.westbowpress.com
844-714-3454

Scriptures are taken from the New King James Version®. Copyright © 1982 by Thomas Nelson. Used by permission. All rights reserved.

ISBN: 978-1-6642-9595-7 (sc)
ISBN: 978-1-6642-9594-0 (e)

Library of Congress Control Number: 2023905673

Print information available on the last page.

WestBow Press rev. date: 4/5/2023

To the reader in a desperate straight, depressing depth, or spiritual maze. What God did for me, He will do for you. There is a truth, there is a power, there is a love that can change your life. Many veterans came back from the Vietnam War, or just served in that era, with wounds and scars—some could be seen and some couldn't, both physical and emotional. Many people also have wounds and scars from the everyday war of life. These few words are dedicated to you.

Contents

Chapter 1   Olive Drab, One Each 1

Chapter 2   Johnny Walker Red 7

Chapter 3   "Is this the real life? Is this just fantasy?" 11

Chapter 4   The Gentle Tyrant 15

Chapter 5   Believing Is Seeing 19

Chapter 6   I Will Not Be a Silly Selma 22

Chapter 7   No Fear (Yeah, Right) 27

Chapter 8   Shut Down and Restart 31

Chapter 9   God Is Invisible 35

Chapter 10   Moral of the Story 38

Chapter 11   To Whom It May Concern 41

Chapter One

OLIVE DRAB, ONE EACH

━━━━━◇━━━━━

I t was March 4, 1969, in a plane over Vietnam, about midnight. Probably midnight. We had been following the sun after leaving Travis Air Force Base in California and landing somewhere in Alaska for fuel, so it's hard to be sure what time it was—or what day it was—because at some point, we stopped being on United States of America time and unknowingly transitioned to Southeast Asia time.

It may not have been midnight on my wristwatch, but it was midnight in my soul. There was loud talking on the flight, mostly new GIs laughing, making crude jokes. But I was silent, alone, and living secretly in my thoughts. I had always been silent and quiet. Self-conscious. Bashful. Fearful.

We were surprised when the lights went out in the cabin. No aisle lights, no overhead lights, no wing lights. Dark. And silent. Still. Suddenly, all our thoughts were focused on the same thing—our future. We were approaching Da Nang Air Base, and the lights were turned out to hide us from enemy fire. No more laughing and joking. Some of us were entering a nightmare. Some of us were approaching our final descent. And perhaps we all joined in a collective, nonverbalized prayer for survival.

Reality set in. This was it. For years, the American public had lived the war from the comfort and security of their living rooms, watching the killing and mayhem on TV in between sitcoms and variety shows. Listening to the daily body counts. I didn't think I would be coming home alive.

Army basic training had been the worst eight weeks of my life. It also got me into the best physical shape of my life. The training they had me do, difficult and impossible for me on many levels, but you didn't think about whether you could do it—you just did it. I made no friends or gained any self-confidence. I only missed home. There was no "I'm doing this for my country. I'm fighting communism for freedom." No one I knew thought like that. No, even though I enlisted when I got my draft notice, I was on that plane because I had to be.

There was no sleep. When we landed—safely, thank you, Lord—we were transported to Long Bien, where we would be cataloged, profiled, uniformed into jungle fatigues, and assigned to our individual duty locations. I ended up near a little village called Di An. My home for the next year was to be the First Infantry Division. "The Big Red One," so called for the red numeral 1 on the patch of our dress greens.

I was an average typist, I guess. I learned to type from the instruction booklet, which came with our little portable Remington Quiet Writer. But when I filled out the questionnaire on my personal history section, I lied just a little (!) and wrote down I could type one hundred words a minute. That was enough to impress the specialist reading it, who was probably a draftee himself doing the interview.

Either that or else he was just a regular guy like me with no experience in human resources, or hiring or firing, or job qualifications, who had no clue if one hundred words a minute was impressive or not. Anyway, it did get me a job as a clerk-typist in the First Infantry Division Support Command, a brigade-level headquarters commanded by a full-bird colonel, one notch below a general. Later, I would impress him with my attention to detail, perfection, and military bearing. Who would have thought?

There were battalions below the brigade and companies below the battalions. Unknown to me, God was working behind the scenes, not only to protect me, but also to arrange good things for me. Not only would He get me through Vietnam, but in one year I got two promotions, a Bronze Star Medal and an Army Commendation Medal for service—without loading a gun. In fact, when I turned in my weapon, M-16, there was a cobweb in the barrel—at least that's the way I remember it.

But back on that first night in country, I hadn't even been issued a weapon when there was a "red alert," which meant that attack was imminent. I made my way to the bunker closest to me, but it was full. No room in the inn. I tried another one—no vacancy. Finally, I just sat down and leaned against a sandbag-covered wall and waited for death ... or at least shooting to begin. But nothing happened that night.

I was put on guard duty. My body still hadn't caught up with the sun. I didn't know what day it was. I could barely hold my eyes open. The sergeant saw my eyes slowly closing and warned me, "Don't go to sleep. You can get court-martialed." Eventually, he let me lie down on a cot with no covers. I fell instantly into a deep sleep.

Something happened that first week, which would impact my life forever. I would never be the same, and it would take me years to recover from it. It wasn't the Vietcong; it wasn't the North Vietnamese Army. It was a cold can of Budweiser.

It was very hot, and I was very thirsty that night. No one in my hooch, a military term for a thatched hut, had any water. I visited our neighbor hooches, and nobody there had any water either. But they all had little refrigerators well stocked with beer. So I drank the beer. And drank the beer.

I hadn't been a drinker before the Army. It sucked me into a downward vortex, from churchgoing, relative normalcy into an abyss of bar-going un-normalcy. We worked seven days a week and partied seven nights a week. Sometimes a party with a bunch of homesick buddies, and sometimes just an intimate party with one of my best friends and me. We'd sit on top of a water tower we had climbed in the middle of a tipsy night, singing oldies but goodies to the moon. I think it was the moon. "There's a moon out tonight, oh, oh, oh, oh."

There was an enlisted men's club, where you could buy booze and beer and occasionally see a live Vietnamese rock band. In the officers' club, there were strippers. We would try to stay out of the way of grunts who had been drafted unwillingly into this "fight to save democracy." They would come in from the real war, dirty and muddy, angry, and looking for trouble.

I traded a beer bottle for a glass of rum and Coke before graduating to scotch on the rocks when I got back to the States. That was about the only thing I graduated from, having dropped out of college, which was what got me my draft notice in the first place and invited out of law school years later. To my joy, I discovered that beer and rum numbed the shyness I had fought all my life. Soon I would try marijuana for the first time, and it latched hold onto my soul and wouldn't let go for years. After all, I reasoned, I wasn't going to be going home alive anyway. God's grace kept me from trying any harder drug, or this story would have had a much different ending.

I excelled at my job assignment despite the drinking. I enjoyed it and was good at it. My superior officers liked my diligence and efficiency. The only battle action I saw was when a VC sniper-fired a few rounds into our office.

President Nixon visited our base one time. One of my friends got to be his jeep driver, and the president gave him an official ink pen. The helicopters would land across the road from our office. Hueys. Cobra gunships. I got to ride in a Huey one time as we ferried our commanding officer (CO) to Saigon for his date with a nurse. He logged air miles for that one. If they got enough miles, they would get another medal of some kind.

Yeah, most of my superiors liked me. Except for our command sergeant major, the highest ranking enlisted man. He didn't like that I had a Vietnamese girlfriend. No, we didn't date or even kiss, but we were an item. She cleaned the office and prepared coffee and Kool-Aid for the officers. Sergeant Major said, when she was there, I didn't get any work done. That was not true.

He would fire her, and I would hire her back. There was a fenced-off "pen," where Vietnamese would wait to be hired by the Army for various jobs. I would approach the fence, and all the girls would rush forward, hoping to be lucky enough to get a job. All but one. She just sat quietly in humble assurance, knowing I had come for her. All the women would just turn and look at her and knowingly say, "Ah."

As I said, we didn't date. When she finished her job, she would take the bus back to her little village, where she lived in a very modest house with her family. Sometimes I would buy cigarettes for her dad from the PX (post exchange), a no-no.

One time I boldly visited her. The village of Di An was strictly off-limits. A couple of buddies dropped me off in the jeep. They drove up the road and turned around and came back by to see if I was all right. I waved. I had no weapon—it wouldn't seem respectful. Love, ignorance, maybe, but this year was to be a surreal adventure. I'm ashamed to say she fixed me a special meal I couldn't eat. After a short stay, chaperoned, I hitchhiked back to the base.

Care packages came from home, with cookies cushioned by popcorn, which we also ate. Letters from Mom and Dad and my sister Pat. To them, I probably sounded the same as when I left, but inside, I was changing.

When my time got short, and I started looking forward to going home, I woke up one morning with a strange feeling, which I had never experienced before. It was like I wasn't really there, like I wasn't really anywhere. Reporting to sick call, the doctor told me it was something he regularly sees—I was depressed to be going home. Told you it was strange. He prescribed antidepressants, and I was okay.

A buddy and I were going home on the same day, only on a different flight, from Long Bien. We passed the waiting hours in a bar, getting drunk. After a while, he looked at his watch, only to discover he had missed his flight. I wonder whatever happened to him.

That year's worth of adventure in Vietnam, I was to discover a boldness, fearlessness, and confidence I had never experienced before nor since. I guess when you think you're going to die anyway, and you've lived a very sheltered life, you roll the dice. The other thing, of course, was the "King of Beers" and his big brother, whiskey. I found that as my blood-alcohol level went up, my inhibition level went correspondingly down. No more crippling, paralyzing shyness.

I was cool.

Chapter Two

JOHNNY WALKER RED

———◇———

Having made it safely through one year of drinking school, Southeast Asia campus, avoiding death and mayhem, with my only injury being the metamorphosis of my soul, I was rudely welcomed home on the ride from Travis Air Force Base to Los Angeles. The bus in which we were being transported collided with a car, and we were left standing by the side of the road, waiting for another bus. No one was injured, but we all agreed how ironic it would have been to be killed our first day back in a freeway accident.

We were further welcomed home by insults and attitude from a "thankful" nation. Everybody hated the war. Especially us.

At my duty station, Armed Forces Entrance and Examination Station in Oakland, California, where I would serve out my final fourteen months of military service, we always changed from our uniforms into civilian clothes before leaving for home. The streets weren't safe. One day someone put a bomb in the U.S. Mail box in front of our building. It blew out the windows, but again, no one was injured.

When my Army days were ending, I had to enter that building

one more time to sign paperwork, and I had to cross a picket line who were determined that I couldn't go in. But I was this close to being free, and no long-haired hippies would stop me. They didn't.

When I finally did get home to my mom and dad's house, they must have thought it strange that I wanted to share with them the new music reel-to-reel tapes (Do you possibly remember them?) I had discovered in Nam. *Inna-Godda-Da-Vida* and other gems. The music group Bread, which I still like, as a matter of fact.

They thought it strange, I'm sure, when I'd come home from bars at closing time, only to go out once again at three or four in the morning, because a beautiful young waitress I had fallen in love with at first sight had called me. I was able to make the trip from La Mirada to Santa Ana without incident or accident, turning up the volume on the Beatles' "Here Comes the Sun."

Yeah, I was still cool. Never mind that Mom and Dad wondered who was sleeping in my bed and wearing my clothes. I had thirty days' leave when I got home, and I spent those nights at the Ritmo, where my sister and her husband worked the bar. My sister's coworker would be my first wife.

Even though I wasn't new, by this time, to drinking, I was new to the bar scene. I didn't even know you were supposed to tip the waitress. That didn't stop this girl who had stolen my heart from going out with me. A miracle, I thought! She made it clear that she was going to continue to date the trumpet player, but I didn't care. I was stricken, one step above smitten. Two months later, we were married. We moved into an apartment in San Leandro, California, she and me and her beautiful four-year-old daughter.

Somewhere between drive-in movies, *Night of the Living Dead*, and night clubs in San Francisco's Jack London Square, we conceived another beautiful daughter.

It was she who would some years later lead me back to church. At first, she would say, as a little girl, "Let's go to Bob Irby's auditorium." Bob Irby was the name of the preacher of the Cypress Church of Christ. Then after some time, she said, "Let's place membership at the church." We did. And that part of my soul story comes later.

Oh, love is a medicine given in doses. Love is a wine, measured by the glass. Love is a tear, squeezed from the heart.

My childhood dream was to become a lawyer, inspired and motivated, I suppose, by old television shows like *The Defenders*, in which justice was always noble; *Perry Mason*, in which justice always won.

So when I got home from Vietnam, owned my first house, had a dependable job, and was surrounded by family love, I went to law school. Since I hadn't finished college and had no degree, I had to take an equivalency test, which I passed.

It was night school. Had to take ten units, which was considered full time. I got a student loan to add to my credit card bills. In orientation, the speaker said, "Look around you. One of the people on either side, their marriage will end in divorce. This is a hard thing you've chosen to do." I was to be the one.

So I carried mail eight hours a day, took classes at night. Somewhere in between, I managed to study. But I needed energy.

My wife had told me, "You don't have any friends, you need a friend." I'm good at following directions, so I got a friend at work. No, it's not what you're thinking; it wasn't a woman.

My new friend turned me on to something called amphetamines. We called them "whites." I bought them by the "jar," which was a plastic bag full of one thousand little pills. When I was down to half a bag, I started worrying about getting my next jar. I had found the energy I needed.

Trouble is the energy lasted into the night. I couldn't sleep. Just so happened, my friend also had access to another drug— pot. I started buying other plastic bags—"lids." Not only did the marijuana help me sleep, but it was fun too. And when you mixed it with Johnnie Walker Red, or Bacardi rum, or Canadian Club, you had a party on your hands. Or at least what a subdued, conservative, shy poet could classify as a party.

Law school was easy for me. At first. Then it got harder, and my study time got shorter. I took my final test in my second year high on pot. It sounded profound when I wrote the test, but the grader didn't agree, and my legal career was over.

I spent the next thirty years hating my job carrying mail. I didn't call what I wore a uniform. I called it a costume. I knew it wasn't me. I knew I was created for more.

Although I hadn't attended church for years, I started a sincere search for God.

Chapter Three

"IS THIS THE REAL LIFE? IS THIS JUST FANTASY?"

—"Bohemian Rhapsody," Queen

Three of us were on the I-5 Santa Ana Freeway from La Mirada, California, to Studio City to see Kenny Kingston, "the psychic to the stars." Of course, we were smoking some pot on the way but nothing unusually potent. God was my copilot many times during my "high" life, although I didn't know it. And if I had known it, I wouldn't have cared. Thank you, Lord.

In fact, I've had to thank God endlessly for the job I cursed for thirty years. I found out you call that "repenting."

I was excited to be dipping into the supernatural, wading in it, seeing how deep I could go.

My partners from the post office, including the friend whom I've already introduced you, weren't as fascinated by the occult as I was. I think they just thought it would be a cool adventure or something different to do. Kenny Kingston had the reputation and notoriety of giving accurate "psychic readings." Movie stars and famous people sought him out.

He was going to be hosting or presenting what could best be described as a "psychic church service," where other-world power would be manifested. What was behind the veil of reality would be revealed. Mystery for the initiated.

I wasn't driving. It was night.

The venue was a relatively small room or hall, rented from a lodge of some kind. There was an American flag up front, and we started with the Pledge of Allegiance. We sang a hymn or two. It was then I had my first metaphysical experience.

I started feeling a tangible, physical "something," an energy. A presence? Then it was as if the ceiling opened to the night sky, and I could see into the universe. As I looked at individual faces, it was like I could see the essence of who they really were, like I could see them separated from their personalities. Like I could see their souls.

The "vibes" got so intense, I had to get up from my seat and find the rest room to escape from the overwhelming sense of—of whatever it was. A couple of minutes later, one of my fellow reality travelers joined me in my refuge. He asked if I was okay, and before I could answer, he said, "I feel it too."

After a bit of regaining composure and feeling somewhat normal again, we went back to the little auditorium, where the folding chairs had been arranged in circles. Various psychics were giving readings to individuals waiting their turn. Each would receive a message from a "spirit guide" or some mystical impression, some secret knowledge from a sixth sense. We joined a group.

To this day, I do not remember any word my "medium" had delivered to me, but I do remember vividly what did happen to me in the circle.

"Luck" sat me next to a young lady about my age. She was pretty but not beautiful, and I felt no attraction toward her. I was too wrapped up in my own private excitement to pay her too much attention, and I wasn't a very social person anyway, so no thought for conversation occurred to me.

But it did to her. "I've dreamed of you," she said. I innocently thought she was coming on to me, as in "You're the man of my dreams." But she wasn't. I literally had been in her dreams—she recognized me.

When she asked me my name and I answered her, she glanced at her friend sitting next to her, and they gave each other a knowing look.

She spoke again, matter-of-factly. "I had a reading recently, and it was predicted that I would marry twice, but my last name would only change once." She showed me her driver's license, and her last name was the same as mine.

My own marriage was on thin ice, and I heard it crack.

Fate or coincidence or karma or just the Twilight Zone, my world did a tilt, and I told my friends to go on home without me. I'd stay up here in la-la land and see what would happen next. "How will you get home?" I didn't know. Or care.

Fortunately, they were very good friends and wouldn't let me be completely insane. We went back together. I had strayed into a supernatural shadow. There really was "another side." There really were "powers." That part is still true.

She gave me her phone number, and I called her several times. "You've got to get out of the house," I heard her say as I stood in the phone booth. As I've said, I'm good at following directions.

Before I left, one night my wife and I were lying in bed. I wasn't asleep. It was dark, but as I looked to the doorway, I saw a shadowy figure approaching the foot of the bed. It seemed to be female. I learned later that demonic angels frequently take that form.

I kind of blinked and shook my head a little, and it disappeared.

There is a saying that the devil will "take you further than you want to go, keep you longer than you want to stay, and cost you more than you want to pay." I was the metal ball in the pinball machine of life. One flipper sent me here, and one flipper sent me there, and I never got a free game. A lot of bells and lights. Satan kept giving me quarters.

My greatest regret is that "GAME OVER" affected not just me, but the people I loved most.

How wonderful it is to know that pinball machine can be unplugged.

Before I could figure that out and come to my senses, our family was broken up. There were a lot of reasons, but I did it. Shoulda, woulda, coulda.

I never finished law school, never finished college, but in the course of time, I did finish school of ministry, finished a men's training class, which really turned me around when I finally got back to church.

Although educators had told my mom and dad I had a genius IQ and put me in special classes at school, I never was able to fit in after eighth grade. Maybe that was one of the reasons drinking and getting high made me feel better at the first.

I was a square peg in a round hole most of my life, it seems. I wonder if everyone feels that way at some time.

"A man or a woman who is a medium or who has familiar spirits shall surely be put to death; they shall stone them with stones. Their blood shall be upon them," Leviticus 20:27.

Chapter Four

THE GENTLE TYRANT

———◇———

I had recently blown out nine candles on my own birthday cake in my childhood home in Arvada, Colorado. Now I had been invited to a birthday party up the street for one of my friends. Winter in Colorado is cold and snowy and dark early. Nighttime was never a friendly time, except when my dad was tucking me in and telling me stories of his own childhood on the farm in Oklahoma and, of course, his war stories from World War 2.

A bunch of us kids were playing in their basement. Suddenly, a sense of loneliness swept over me, and I didn't want to be there. I wanted to be home. I sneaked into the little room where our coats were, found mine, and without telling anyone, I hurried back down the block to *away*.

Somewhere close to that period, I was lying on my twin bed one night, at the end of what I remember to be an ordinary day. Suddenly, I felt a pressure, as if a "presence" had laid down on top of me. I didn't know what it was, but it scared me. It remained, so I called out to Mom, whose room was down the hall. Dad worked nights. I needed some kind of touch of reality, so I called out to her. "Mom, what time does Dad get home?"

"Same time as always, one o'clock. You know that."

After a while, the weight was gone.

Mom and Dad fought a lot. In junior high, I became self-conscious, insecure, lonely, and depressed.

Edgar Allan Poe was my favorite poet and author. Every new school year, when we received our new books, I would expectantly flip through the literature book to see if there was a Poe. His melancholy style spoke to my heart, expressed my heart. I can still quote from "The Raven," after all these years.

The best compliment a teacher ever gave me was from my tenth-grade English teacher. On one of my short stories, which I had written not as an assignment but just for pleasure, he wrote, "Excellent. You are the Edgar Allan Poe of the 20th Century."

My dream/goal was to publish a book by the time I was twenty-one. Didn't happen. A couple of rejection slips from magazines was enough to discourage me.

In my twenties, I was still writing, adding songs to my body of unpublished, unrecognized, unshared expressions of my soul. Even if I started out writing happy lyrics, by the last verse, it had turned into a country song. Some of the songs were good.

By the time my drinking days were in full swing, I owned three guitars, a banjo, and a portable recording studio, where I was able to tape myself singing a four-part harmony to my original music. I copyrighted much of my work, just in case future generations should discover "L. A. Long."

L. A. Long was my "stage name." Under that name, I self-published a book of poetry titled *The Gentle Tyrant*, which was a name that a psychic had once called me during a reading.

One time my roommate gave a party at our apartment. One of the guests never left, just stayed. And stayed. He was a songwriter too, and eventually, my original roommate moved out.

We dreamed of stardom, smoked pot, and drank beer. The closest we came to Entertainer of the Year was a couple of open-mic nights at bars. I had several shots to summon the courage to get up on that stage. I had discovered stage fright in seventh-grade drama class, and it was my constant curse for decades.

As for my duet partner, I came home from work one day to find him and his girlfriend shooting up heroin in our dining room. In a few years, he would die too young, and he was soon out of my life after that episode.

God protected me from the hard stuff. Once, I did drop some acid, LSD, at a baseball game in Angel Stadium, but it scared me so badly, I was never tempted again.

God had His hands full, protecting me in those days. As you are reading this, I wonder if you are aware of His hand on your shoulder. I wonder if you are aware that He has thoughts and plans for you, for a future and a hope. Angels are real.

One night I was lying on my bed, looking around at all the many books I had accumulated and studied in my search for truth. There were books on metaphysics, mysticism, Eastern religions, self-hypnosis, candle-burning, the occult.

As I looked at the rows of commentary on the supernatural, I realized I had no Bible. Not one. No King James, no New King James. Nothing. I prided myself on being a truth-seeker, a student of truth, and I had no Bible. So I stole one from my dentist.

No, I didn't really steal it. He had a paperback Bible in the waiting room with a sticker on it that said, "Take me home." So I did.

It was my personal Bible for quite a while.

Dad was always telling me, "You go to all these seminars and classes, why don't you come back to church?"

I would say, "On Sundays, I just want to read my paper and drink my six-pack."

He said, "I've discovered this preacher on TV. He's different. You've got to check him out." Mom and Dad were diehard Church of Christer's, so for him to say that was unthinkable.

After watching the preacher once, I started recording every

program on tape, no VCR yet. The Bible came to life in a new, thrilling—yes, thrilling!—way. It was real. Not just words printed on a page, but it was also the Word of God! Contrary to what they taught me in two and a half years of college, God was not dead!

Chapter Five

BELIEVING IS SEEING

———⸢◇⸥———

There were four hundred houses on my mail route, four hundred porches I had to climb up and down every day. Halfway through one of those summer days, my supervisor pulled up in his personal car. Not a good sign in a climate of "snooper-vison."

Dad had been taken to the hospital with a heart attack. I drove back to the post office and deposited my leftover mail then rushed to be with Mom, who was at his bedside.

I prayed with Dad just before they wheeled him away to have some kind of test done. He had been taking heart medicine for years, and the doctor told us he was afraid of what he might find.

To the doctor's surprise—shock, really—not only was there no indication of a heart attack, but there also appeared to be no physical evidence of any scar tissue or anything that would indicate that he ever had heart issues. Dad was released and was permanently taken off the heart medication.

Thank you, Lord. I believe in prayer.

After I had been restored to fellowship with God, and for years had been active in church leadership, I got a call from the church office, asking me to make a ministry visit to Children's Hospital in Los Angeles.

I'm ashamed to say I didn't want to go. I was still masquerading as a mailman, always tired at the end of the day, and I hated driving in Los Angeles. But I never tell God no. I told him no for too many years because of insecurity and fear. So no, I don't think I seriously considered not going. I'm so glad.

I wasn't given any information about the patient or any diagnosis. I was surprised and touched as I walked into the hospital room to see a little boy hooked up to wires and tubes, with his young mother sitting, leaning over his bed.

He was four years old and in a coma. His mother was staying at Ronald McDonald House, as they were from Arizona. She told me the doctors didn't know what was wrong with him and that he had hours to live. If I had known all that, my attitude when I got the request would have been much different. But then fear and self-doubt might have set in too, battling my faith.

He wasn't aware of my presence, but I leaned over him, lightly placed my hand on his shoulder, and said, "Hello, TJ. My name is Larry. I'm a grandpa. I'm going to pray for you."

I stood on one side, his sobbing momma on the other. Usually, when I pray for someone like that, I hold the loved one's hand as I pray. But this time his mother threw herself over her son's quiet body, and I said a short prayer.

When we were finished, she walked me to the elevator, rode down with me, and I'll never forget the emotion with which she whispered to me, "You're not going to leave us, are you? You will be back."

I promised I would, and I did. Several times over the next few days, I drove the dreaded route to Los Angeles, only my attitude had changed. We had made a connection. This wasn't religious theory or magic formulas; this was truth in action. Reality truth. God truth and God love. TJ and Momma were real people in real crisis.

One evening, as I walked into their room, I was shocked. There he was, awake and playing some kind of game on his bed tray. Next time I came I brought him some crayons. Next time I came he had been released.

Thank you, Lord.

Another time I was called to the hospital to pray for another young mother, at least she hoped to be a mother. She and her husband had suffered several miscarriages. I had to wash up thoroughly and wear surgical gown and gloves and mask to enter her room.

As I prayed, it's hard to explain, but I felt in my heart an intense love for that unborn child. The words came easily, and after some days, she gave birth to a healthy baby.

Thank you, Lord.

"If you ask anything in My name, I will do it" John 14:14.

Chapter Six

I WILL NOT BE A SILLY SELMA

———◆———

aving rediscovered church on a visitor-only basis, I was rehearsing in my apartment with the other half of my wannabe singer-songwriting team, "Buck and L.A.," of which I've already told you about, when there was a knock at the door. I put down my guitar and Bud. It was a couple of guys from church. They were actually "missionaries" from another state, who were working with the local church my daughter and I were attending.

I was too embarrassed to invite them in, but we had a brief discussion at the door. They said my beliefs were "interesting." I was a little impressed with them, although I can't put my finger on exactly why. Never saw them again. But they watered a spiritual seed that had been planted by the TV preacher.

In that particular denomination (if they heard me call them a "denomination," I'd be taken out behind the barn), when you had been away from the church, away from God like the prodigal son, the way you showed your repentance was to get out of your seat and walk down to the front of the congregation during the "invitation song," where you would be prayed for and "restored to fellowship." It took all the courage I had, and I almost didn't make it before the last chorus of the song finished, but there I went, trembling and sweating. Welcome home!

The church in which we were regular visitors was in walking distance of my mom and dad's house. But Dad recommended we start attending another church, whose minister Mom and Dad used to know. A very good suggestion, it turned out. We started attending the other church.

To say it was a good suggestion is a gross understatement because it turned my life around super dramatically.

I was content to sit on the back row, where I could get out the door fast and not become involved. If I had worn a Superman suit, the big "S" would have stood for "Still Shy. Super Introvert." I was happy to be unseen, unnoticed, and unapproached.

My daughter, on the other hand, wanted to become a part of this church family. Another tradition they have is that when you want to join the church, you walk down front during the song and "place membership." My little girl said, "Let's place membership." Another "good" suggestion. Another understatement. Thank heaven for little girls. I wonder what she knew way back then—did the Holy Spirit speak through her pure heart?

My first memory of church is darkness. Physical darkness. Lying on an unpadded wooden pew, with my head in Mom's lap, I could hear rustling of hymn book pages, coughing in the distance, a baby crying somewhere. I could hear whispering from the row behind us, my mom's alto voice in a cappella congregational singing, and dad trying to sing bass.

I couldn't hold my eyes open. They hurt. My eyes gave me a lot of trouble in my early years. I couldn't finish kindergarten because they watered so much.

Mornings found them stuck closed. I couldn't stretch them open, no matter how hard I tried. Mom would bathe them with a "wash rag" soaked in a boric acid solution until slowly I could open them. Whether that was an old-wives'-tale-treatment passed down from Granny or a remedy she invented, I never knew. Maybe she got it from the same source of medical knowledge that told us we couldn't play in the water hose in summer because that caused polio. At any rate, the technique worked for me.

Kids like to play "blind man's bluff" with me because I had a natural blindfold.

Mom and Dad took me to every eye specialist in Los Angeles. That's the way I heard my dad tell the story countless times over the years. Not one doctor could cure me or even diagnose me.

Even though Dad was raised in church, in a small country town in Oklahoma, he had fallen away after World War 2. But he made a deal with God, like so many of us do. He said, "God, if you heal my son's eyes, I will go back to church." God did, and Dad did.

When I was about four years old, a doctor advised Mom and Dad to move from California to Colorado because when we were back there on vacation, visiting my mother's sister, my eyes were okay. So they immediately sold the house at a major loss, and we moved.

It didn't take long for my eyes to go bad again.

Dad got a job as soon as we moved, and his new boss suggested he take me to a chiropractor he knew. Dad didn't believe in such doctors, but he believed in keeping his job, so he called this guy up.

The chiropractor told Dad he wasn't taking any new cases. Dad said, "That's okay, I don't believe in chiropractors anyway. I've had my son to every eye specialist in Los Angeles, and they couldn't do anything, so I know you couldn't either."

The way my dad told the story, the chiropractor said, "Wait a minute. You say you've had him to every eye doctor in LA? I'll tell you what, you bring him in. And if I can't help him, you won't owe me a cent."

As I remember it, the doctor was old, and his office was in an old house we had to climb under a fence to get to.

Dad started to tell him my symptoms, but the doctor stopped him and said, "Don't tell me his symptoms, I will tell you." So Mr. Chiropractor proceeded to examine me and then told Mom and Dad all my symptoms: nose bleeds, eyes stuck and watery, all of it. He said my problem was that my optic nerve had been damaged, almost severed, at birth. He took my parents aside and spoke quietly to them. I only remember one treatment, but it was painful as he adjusted—cracked—my neck.

God had arranged providentially to have our family move halfway across the country, cause my dad to be hired by a boss who just happened to know a doctor, and to have that doctor be one who loved a challenge to prove the validity of his profession. Holy Spirit playing chess, moving all the pieces to their best possible, most strategic positions.

Thank you, Lord.

When I was finally able to resume school, I made up for lost time. Learning came easily for me, and I excelled faster and further than my friends. And I was the class clown.

Many times I had to write a hundred times, "I will not be a Silly Selma."

Until the symphony.

Exposed and naked like in a public humiliation dream, that's how my prepubescent psyche felt as I stood in front of two successive classrooms, apologizing. I had minutes earlier stood before the school principal, my first experience at being "bad" at school. I was one of "them." Was I really? I didn't feel bad, but I must be.

On a field trip to a real symphony, a very dignified experience, I'm told, I was cutting up, as was my style, and making people laugh. The principal didn't think it was funny. He called me the "ringleader." My first conspiracy and I wasn't even aware of it. So off to my apology tour down the halls.

I did apologize to two classes. Up in front of them. In my head, I heard their derision and ridicule. I was, indeed, very sorry, sorry this was actually happening to me. I pictured Mom and Dad being hurt and disappointed that their "perfect" son had disgraced them.

All this, of course, was magnified and distorted by my young imagination. But my "Silly Selma" days were over. My self-conscious, low self-esteem, un-normal personality was born.

Years from then, Vietnam would give me the antidote to that poison, to be taken by the six-pack.

Chapter Seven

NO FEAR (YEAH, RIGHT)

Just as the Holy Spirit directed our way to the healing of my eyes, so He directed my daughter and me to the best church for the healing of my shyness. Several members of that small church probably didn't realize it, but they made a move on my chess board of life. Not the least of whom was our preacher, who started a "men's training class."

Another was a man who taught a small adult Sunday school class, who taught me a very important Scripture, which has stayed with me all these years: "If anyone speaks, let him speak as the oracles of God. If anyone ministers, let him do it as with the ability which God supplies ... " (1 Peter 4:11 NKJ).

At the time, both to speak and to minister were so far beyond what I believed possible. I couldn't even imagine it. But that verse became a magnet, drawing me toward God and the plans He had for me.

God's power, God's Word, energized me and motivated me, leading me into the arena of fear, which I had done everything in my power to avoid all those years.

It was fear that got me to Vietnam. I had been a letter-carrier for the post office less than a year when I got my draft notice. I had lost my 2-S college deferment when I dropped out of college. So to avoid the infantry, I enlisted, choosing to go to the Army Intelligence School in Baltimore, Maryland. I could see myself being a spy. *The Man from U.N.C.L.E.*, *I Spy*. Right.

School was almost finished. I had my picture taken for my special agent badge. However, there was one more class. I would have to interrogate a subject, suspect, in front of the class! I couldn't, I refused to do it. Too scared of being in front of the class. Was that from being on a Silly Selma apology tour?

I seriously contemplated placing my hand on the local railroad track, but I didn't have the nerve for that either. So I took the bus to Downtown Baltimore, sat in the bus station, and composed an anonymous letter to the commanding officer accusing me of something that would get me kicked out of school.

It didn't exactly work as I planned, but I didn't have to get up in front of the class. Instead, I got sent to Vietnam—in the First Infantry Division.

So I didn't finish intelligence school or college or law school. But thank you, Lord, for the men's training class, which I did finish.

I was petrified when I got up to speak that first time in the class. In our church, regular men, not pastors or preachers or professionals, just laymen, led church services. Except for Sunday sermons, men from the congregation led the worship singing, the communion service, Sunday school, and Wednesday evening devotionals. This particular class was to train men to do all that.

Maybe a dozen of us showed up. On our first trial run, our first assignment was to stand up front for two to five minutes, talk about our favorite Scripture. I hadn't been a serious Bible student long enough to have a favorite verse. When we played a game called "Bible trivial pursuit," I was not a star or scholar. But we had just heard a sermon on John 10:10, so I chose that.

"The thief does not come except to steal and to kill and to

destroy. I have come that they may have life and that they may have it more abundantly" (NKJ).

How fearful I was! All the shyness, all the stage fright that had shackled me all my life, all came to bear on my mind and body that night.

In subsequent years, I would come to learn "For God has not given us a spirit of fear but of power and of love and of a sound mind" (2 Timothy 1:7). Spirit of fear, of timidity, of cowardice, I could identify and define what I had called "shyness" and "being bashful" all those years. So it was a spirit. Aha!

Something inside me told me I needed to do it. Not a whisper, but a nudging, a pulling. I would do it—for God. It was only that thought that kept me from refusing the podium that night. God wanted me to do it, something—Someone—said.

I kept my head bowed, not out of reverence, but so that I couldn't see any faces. My voice trembled; my hands shook. All the typical symptoms of stage fright I knew so well, they were there in full force. *But I did it!*

Years later, our preacher who led the class would tell the congregation, "When Larry spoke that first time, I could hardly hear him, and I was in the front pew. Now when he speaks from the pulpit, he doesn't even need a microphone."

Because God wanted me to do it.

"'For I know the plans I have for you,' declares the Lord, 'plans to prosper you and not to harm you, plans to give you hope and a future'" (Jeremiah 29:11 NIV).

The road map that led from the back pew to the pulpit winded through much fear and trepidation but always with the compass pointed north.

Over the years, I had tried self-help books, self-hypnosis, books on public speaking. Nothing helped. Only one motivation started to recreate my inner man—believing I was doing it for God.

The deacon in charge of the worship service (*Lord, note that man and thank him for me.*) recognized I could sing and that I knew a lot about music, so he asked me to lead singing. I carried my stomach of butterflies with me to the front that first time, shaking and trembling all the way. My voice quivered, and I was painfully aware that it was noticeable. I felt completely out of place and in over my head. Unqualified. But God wanted me to do it.

I became the head song leader.

Change the scene to our church auditorium. Twenty or thirty men and women assembled to discuss the upcoming vacation Bible school (VBS). VBS is a weeklong "summer school" for students on recess, from kindergarten age through adult.

I had, by this time, been a VBS teacher, first junior high then college. I was prepared for more of that. I wasn't prepared when the VBS director asked for volunteers for the assistant director position, and the main elder, a professor at Pepperdine University in Malibu, leaned over, looked my way, and pointed his finger at me. My nonacceptance was ignored.

To my dismay, I found out God has a sense of humor, for a week later, the director had to step down, and I had to step up. Thankfully, we had a good team around me, and the school was successful.

I had to step up again when we found ourselves without a preacher. There had been a "church split." One Wednesday night at Bible study, we waited as usual for the announcements to be made. But no one came forward. Awkward pause as I looked around. No one. So I got up from my seat and took over.

Humble confidence and boldness walked with me as I entered a new season in ministry. Because God wanted me to do it.

I began preaching.

After a time, I was offered the position of minister. Unfortunately, I turned it down because my newfound confidence didn't allow that I could prepare two sermons a week and lead the Wednesday night Bible study too.

But a fire had been lit in my spirit.

Chapter Eight

SHUT DOWN AND RESTART

⸻◈⸻

Except for two years, you wouldn't have known it to look at me and my progress, but I was a closet drinker. Liquor and pot and pills had been defeated, but I hadn't been delivered from the King of Beers. Speaking in the pulpit on Sunday and sneaking into the liquor store on Monday.

Two years kept me on the wagon because of the Christian girl I was dating. She broke up with me because we had both been divorced, and church teaching prohibited our being remarried. When she gave me the news, I bought a six-pack, closed myself in my bedroom, and told her in my mind, "This Bud's for you."

"The whole world lies under the sway of the wicked one," 1 John 5:19.

The TV preacher I told you about, I kept reading all his books. He taught something called the "baptism in the Holy Spirit." My daughter and I were living in a small apartment with a walk-in closet. One day I took my beer and his book on "how to receive the Holy Spirit" and sat down in that closet.

There was no trumpet blast, no goose bumps, no ecstasy, but I received the baptism in the Holy Spirit.

I remember, as I led the church in singing the next Sunday, I had them be still and pray silently. While they were doing that, I, myself, was praying quietly in tongues. Were the truth known about that, my acceptance at that church would have been terminated, excommunicated, you might say. They didn't believe in any such thing, nor divine healing, nor the active work of the Holy Spirit.

Once you see a truth, you cannot un-see it.

I was leading the Wednesday night service when we had just changed the starting time from 7:30 p.m. to 7:00 p.m. After the worship and devotional, I began my teaching. I said, "Something's going to happen to disrupt the service tonight because we're going to study things the devil wants kept secret." I didn't have any specific foreknowledge, I just felt like saying it.

Halfway through, at what would have been our old starting time, an older gentleman I didn't know walked in the back door and made his way close to the front. He interrupted me several times until I told him, "If you have any questions, talk to me after we're finished."

When we said our "Amen," he was up out of his seat in a flash, got in my face, and as he was so agitated, as he talked to me, he spit, "You're making these people worse than infidels."

I had taught on prayer. Mark 11:24, "Therefore I say to you, whatever things you ask when you pray, believe that you receive them, and you will have them."

I found out, when he left, that he was the founding elder of that church. He had helped start the congregation.

I realized then that I would not be able to go very far in that denomination. I knew I had to leave. So I started looking for a new church that believed in the full gospel.

At one huge new church we visited, about an hour from our house, a stranger came up to me outside after service, as I munched on a free doughnut, and said, "You know, you're never going to find the perfect church." I kept looking.

In Acts 10 and 11, a man named Cornelius was given direction by an angel, telling him where to go and whom to see, to find someone who would tell him words. Angels are ministering spirits for us (Hebrews 1:14). I wonder if unseen angels lead us today under the direction of the Holy Spirit, to position us in the church body as He pleases.

In all the Bible studies I've led, in my home and in facilities, I wonder if those angels guided the students to hear words.

In case you don't know it, the Holy Spirit is alive and well and actively guides us and speaks to us if we are looking and listening.

"Call to Me, and I will answer you and show you great and mighty things, which you do not know" (Jeremiah 33:3 NKJV).

Somewhere between my old church and my new church, I lost all the progress I had made in public speaking. The timidity had returned. The fear. This time I knew it was a spirit of fear but that knowledge did not help me.

We attended Cottonwood Christian Center several months. Sometimes I sat down in the front row with Colgate on my breath to disguise the beer I had drunk before coming. Keep in mind that sometimes I had to drink a couple of beers to get up the nerve to go into a shop to get my hair cut. I had to drink some liquid nerve to go to our apartment mailboxes because I had to walk by a lot of people at the pool.

Not only was I hooked on Budweiser, but I also had painful bone spurs. That's bad news for a letter-carrier. My podiatrist had tried several things, and he said there was only one thing left to try— injecting my heels with cortisone. I had to sleep with my feet hanging off the end of the bed, but no, thank you, to injections. I would bear it.

I had heard that in our new church—yes, we were planted— there was a school of ministry. I knew immediately that was my next step. Except for one thing. You couldn't be a drinker and become a student there. Oh well.

One night at the regular Sunday-night healing service, the pastor announced he was going to pray for the sick from the pulpit. He said, "If you need healing, raise your hand as I pray. Look around you, and if you see anyone with their hand up, lay your hands on them."

I was too shy to raise my hand, of course, even if it meant being healed. What would people think? Everyone would be looking at me, I was sitting in the second row of a big church.

Wouldn't you know, a lady right in front of me raised her hand. No one moved to put their hand on her. The pastor started praying. Doesn't anyone see this person? She needs healing.

For her, I summoned all my courage and gently placed my hand on her shoulder. I never knew what happened to her, but immediately, I felt a warmth come over me. It started in my face, like a blush, and filled my whole body.

Not all at once, but over the next several days, I lost all desire for beer.

My feet stopped hurting.

Neither condition has ever come back.

Chapter Nine

GOD IS INVISIBLE

(But You Can See Him in Hindsight)

I would not have made it through the Vietnam War without God. I couldn't even visualize myself in a war. Dad had a large catalog of war stories in his memory about World War 2. They would have made a good John Wayne movie. Dad was a raconteur unintentionally. He was skilled at telling stories and thoroughly enjoyed talking. In fact, my mom used to say that before he went to war, he was very quiet, and when he came home, he couldn't stop talking.

I couldn't talk before I went, and I couldn't talk after I went. Unless I had a bottle or glass in my hand. Vietnam did it.

Rather than a John Wayne movie, my war experience was more like the old *M*A*S*H* television series. And no, I wasn't "Radar." I would have seen myself as "Hawkeye."

Even though I was just a clerk and not a fighter, war is war. War is killing and casualties and corpses. War is violence and hate and fear, no matter how noble the cause. I was not equipped physically, mentally, or emotionally to survive, no matter what the draft board would have said to the contrary.

One of my friends in Nam had been a schoolteacher back in the world. When he got to the Big Red One, he was a conservative non-partier devoted to his wife. After he received his "Dear John" letter, he was right there drinking with the best of us and doing worse. He made it home all right, but last I ever heard of him, he had quit his teaching position, bought a motorcycle, and took to the road. The background music you hear is "Born to Be Wild."

At home, there were many things in life I could not do. While in safety and peace, in normalcy and routine, I was immature and insecure, unprepared and unqualified.

I suppose there have been such people as me, who rose to the top in war and became heroes. Others somehow survived by the skin of their teeth. For me, it was the grace of God. I didn't know it at the time, of course. The closest I got to God was when the young lady I told you about got a job at the chapel on base, and I would visit her occasionally, hitchhiking there and back.

In basic training and jungle school, I was always the last in putting my rifle back together after cleaning it, which I also had trouble doing. I was fearful of tossing the live hand grenade in training. The "gas chamber" was more than a challenge but just short of panic. My lungs hurt if I had to run for extended periods, which my drill sergeant loved to make us do. I was intimidated by stronger, coarser personalities.

"I have called you by your name; you are mine. When you pass through the waters, I will be with you; and through the rivers, they shall not overflow you. When you walk through the fire, you shall not be burned, nor shall the flame scorch you. For I am the Lord your God ... " Isaiah 43:1–3.

Vietnam didn't really do it. Southeast Asia was a stage. In my mind, I was the main character. Performing to an audience of whispers and apparitions, I was unaware of the real drama playing behind the curtain. A real-life war saga unfolding scene after scene in heavenly places, as mystical forces dueled for my soul.

Now that I have read the script and am more familiar with the playwright and the director, I am able to read between the lines and anticipate cues. The Bible is the script; the playwright is the author of all things, of course, God.

If I were writing the story, I would have left out Act 2, "Vietnam Did It." But the truth is I did write the second act. And I'm writing Act 3 even now.

I don't know how that act turns out, the details of it. But I do know the epilogue:

"I have fought the good fight, I have finished the race, I have kept the faith. Finally, there is laid up for me the crown of righteousness, which the Lord, the righteous Judge, will give to me on that Day, and not to me only but also to all who have loved His appearing," 2 Timothy 4:7–8.

Chapter Ten

MORAL OF THE STORY

Revolution and Evolution

S ome of you may remember your old Kodak Instamatic. Back
in the days, when you couldn't see what you had just taken a
snapshot of until the film had been developed, days or even
years (procrastinators will understand) later.

I want to say that this book is like that. But I don't know if what
you hold in your hand is the negative or the print. Or maybe it's the
darkroom where the negative film is dipped in trays of developing
fluid.

It is a representation of revolution and evolution. Infancy
to maturity. Rebirth to renewal. Darkness to light. Bondage to
freedom.

Vietnam was a detour on my life's road. It was a roundabout
way to get from point A to point B. It took me from point A to E,
F, and G, and then to B. I guess I'm near C or D now.

If you can remember your Instamatic, then you can remember
the old fold-out road maps, the ones you could unfold but never put
back together. If I had one for my life, I could see where I was born,

where the "war" was, where I am now, and where I want to be. It would even tell me how many miles separated the different points. No map.

No script with stage movements.

No music soundtrack to tell me what my mood should be.

I can tell the difference between the black-and-white negative and the color print. I can feel the changes as I go from one tray to the next. I can see a reflection of reality as the image slowly appears. But it seems like a mystery, doesn't it? If it were a code, how could we decipher it?

There is a secret I want to reveal. Consider yourself initiated so that you are eligible to see it, qualified to receive it, and authorized to activate it.

Here it is: I know the photographer. His name is "God." Not "god." Not a god. Not one of many "gods." God.

A revolution is a sudden, violent overthrow. If it's true for me, it can be true for you. I'm giving you firsthand information I wish I had received before I left point A. Actually, I did receive it, but I ignored it. I didn't comprehend and grasp the utter realness of it.

But what's done is done. While we can't go back, we can go forward. We don't have to stay where we are.

We can have a Saul-to-Paul experience. In the Bible, the New Testament, a man named Saul was persecuting the church, pursuing and imprisoning men and women who believed in Jesus Christ and His resurrection. While on the road to do that very thing, the Lord appeared to him and changed his life completely and forever. Revolution.

When a soldier checked out of Vietnam, there was paperwork to do, rules to follow. We weren't allowed to take certain things home with us. Some diehard rebels did anyway, but I was not one of them. So I only brought home items that were authorized.

Except for one thing.

I brought home an addiction to drinking. Vietnam did it. God un-did it.

You probably didn't have to tour that part of the world, all expenses paid by the U.S. Army. But you have had other battlegrounds. You may be facing an enemy right this very minute. Your road map may be all crumpled up and tossed in the waste basket. Your roll of film, it seems, was exposed to sunlight and is ruined.

God is real. He sees where you're at. He will hear if you call. Your heart as well as your mind are in sending mode. He is always receiving. You just have to tune in.

"'For I know the thoughts that I think toward you,' says the Lord, 'thoughts of peace and not of evil, to give you a future and a hope. Then you will call upon Me, and I will listen to you. And you will seek Me and find Me, when you search for Me with all your heart. I will be found by you,' says the Lord ... " Jeremiah 29:11–14a.

Chapter Eleven

TO WHOM IT MAY CONCERN

———◇———

I was a little guy standing atop a five-foot high brick fence pillar, "preaching" to an imaginary audience, on a small paved road running along the side of Aunt Fan's acreage.

Clenching a pocket New Testament, which I couldn't yet read, I proclaimed the Gospel in kid words I don't remember.

Nor do I recall being aware of the approach of a stranger from my left. But there he was, all of a sudden standing there looking at me. Listening.

His attention was un-welcome and intimidating. I jumped down and ran to the other end of the fence, climbed up with difficulty, and resumed my "sermon."

To my surprise and dismay, the mystery man followed me down the road and stood again in front of me. This time it scared me enough that I leaped off the pillar and ran into the house. Okay, I was no Apostle Paul.

I kept running from public speaking for the next thirty years. But "the gifts and the calling of God are irrevocable" (Romans 11:29).

Bro. Wilfred MacKenzie, the preacher at our little church, a couple of years after that episode, told my proud parents one Sunday, "Someday Larry will be a preacher." Our denomination did not believe in prophecy for today. They probably hadn't even heard about it. Or if they did, they kept it a well-hidden secret.

And those preacher's words might have been just something you say to a boy's mom and dad. But in this case, Brother MacKenzie had a word of wisdom, a word for the future.

The thoughts clumsily expressed through the sincere words of this small book testify that the gift that is in *you*, even if it is concealed and buried under oppressive layers of fear and self-doubt, is real and ready to be exposed.

Exposed—maybe that's the key. You may have to expose your vulnerability. You may have to bring yourself to an assurance that God put that *something* in you. If He put it in you, He trusts you with it.

You may have to turn loose of the side of the pool. Start walking from the shallow end. For someone like me, who can't swim, that is an oh-so-real analogy.

For me, to speak publicly was not merely inching away from three-feet chlorinated water, but it was jumping off the Seal Beach pier into who-knows-what danger.

But like Peter walking on the water, Jesus Himself was there to save me. The Holy Spirit was already in the ocean right below me, waiting for me with a spiritual life preserver. And the Father was whispering, "Jump."

Another book
and Gospel tracts
by this author

The Gentle Tyrant (L. A. Long)

The Young Man
Precious Memories
Foxhole

My body used to take my spirit where it didn't want to go.
Now my spirit takes my body where it is happy to go.

Here are some blank pages on which to start your own story of change.

Printed in the United States
by Baker & Taylor Publisher Services